# Shenell Dixon

All quotes, unless otherwise noted, are from the New King James Version Copyright 1979,1980,1982 by Thomas Nelson, Inc. Used by permission. All rights reserved. Scriptures marked KJV are taken from the Holy Bible, King James Version. Public Domain. Holy Bible, New Living Translation, © copyright 1996, 2004, 2015 by Tyndale House Foundation. Used by permission of Tyndale House Publishers Inc.,

Major In Ministry Minor in Industry
The Fundamentals of Worship

Shenell Dixon Ministry
dixonshenell@gmail.com
shenelldixonministries.com
facebook / Instagram- Shenell Dixon

Copyright © 2019
ISBN: 9781097816002
Cover Design: Shonda Glenn -The Church Whisperer Graphic Designer
Published by: Away of Escape Publishing - statuschangers.com /281-771-9237

# CONTENTS

MAJOR IN MINISTRY
MINOR IN INDUSTRY

# Introduction

*Major In Ministry Minor In Industry* is a Clarion Call for all Worship Leaders to come together, and be Recharged, Reignited, Revived, Refreshed, & Rebuilt.  Worship Leaders aren't restricted to the people that hold mics in their hands.  In this book, we will unpack the Fundamentals of Worship.

I strongly believe that each generation should reach back and help the next generation channel through the things they've been through. Many have questioned my reasoning for hosting the Symposium.  My answer is, I was privileged to have people in my life that cared enough about me to teach me the Basic Fundamentals of Ministry way before they began to cultivate any of my gifts.  I was brought up on teachings such as:

> ➤ "Humble yourself under The Mighty Hand of God."

> ➤ "Don't make people glad twice, glad to see you get up and glad to see you sit down."

> ➤ "Wait on your calling, God will exalt you. It's better to be asked up, than ushered down."

Just to name a few teachings.

I join hands with the generations before me and grab the hands of the generations behind me and say, "Let's bridge the gap and do Ministry well."

I also dedicate this book to the late great *LeAndrew Laron Gaddie* who cared enough about my soul to teach me the *Fundamentals of Worship* before he began to cultivate any of my gifts. Being under his tutelage has taught me how to successfully channel through many doors with grace and obedience to God. The one lesson that stands out the most that he would teach is, "You have to spend time in the Word of God, because without it you cannot Minister to anyone."

I pray that after reading this book, your focus will be centered on building a long-lasting relationship with the Father and being obedient to His Will. Major In Ministry Minor In Industry.

Much Love,
Shenell Dixon

# "Worship Is a Lifestyle"

Shenell Dixon is a Mother, Singer, Song Writer, Recording Artist, Actress, Author, Evangelist, Life Coach, & Biblical Counselor based in Houston, Texas.  In the Summer of 2008, she released her first CD, "Spiritual Jukebox" with her best hits being, "Don't Panic" & "Grateful." There's much more music to come.

She is the Author of her first book entitled, "The Healing Side of Hurt". She introduces this book in efforts to help free people from the stench and residue of hurt and pain.  She's eager to introduce and welcome you to the Healing Side of Hurt.

Shenell Dixon introduced Paradigm Shift in the Fall of 2018, which is a Life Coach and Biblical Counseling Business that help people safely channel through the processes in life.

In the Spring of 2019, Shenell will be hosting a Praise & Worship Symposium entitled Major In Ministry Minor In Industry on May 18th, 2019 @ The Luke Church 2380 S Houston Ave. Humble, Texas. She will release her second book, which is dedicated to all Worshippers also entitled, ***"Major In Ministry Minor In Industry: The Fundamentals Of Worship."***

Shenell spends her leisure time cooking, singing, traveling, writing songs, reading, and being a Mother to her Awesome Children, Amber & Tyler Dixon.

# What Is Worship?

## *Chapter 1*

This is truly the #QOTD (Question of the Day) that's asked by many. Before we begin to unpack such a loaded question, let's begin at its definition. Worship is defined as an extreme form of love — it's a type of unquestioning devotion. Simply put, worship is, anything you put your heart and affection in. This is an individualized expression that is formed out of interest and/or gratitude. Worship isn't an observing event. It's a lifestyle to be lived. While Worship is an outward expression, it's also an inward feeling that transforms the worshiper into the image of the One Worshiped. When you think about Worship and it being such an outpouring of limitless gratitude, you must find something worthy of such adoration.

*"You don't get to decide to worship.*
*Everyone worships something.*
*The only choice you get is what to*
*worship"*
*- Timothy Keller*

Worth is defined as the level at which someone or something deserves to be valued or rated.

Oftentimes, we weigh our worth solely based on our achievements, performance, or visible perceived gifts. Because worth is determined according to our mental perception of what's being weighed, we can't Worship anything that we don't deem weighty enough to Worship. This is similar to the way that we weigh the worth of God. There's a saying that states, "This doesn't hold any weight." It's a common colloquialism used to determine worth. In my years of experience of Worship, one major lesson I've learned is that, people will Worship you according to what they have attached to you and how they weigh you.

I used to get so frustrated and upset when the congregation wouldn't participate in Worship, until I learned that one can't Worship what they have not experienced. You can Minister about anything; however, their response will indicate what they know about Him. True worship depends solely on the mental grip that they have of who God really is to them. How can you properly worship something or someone if you know nothing about them? God designed for us to know Him individually. Corporate Worship is great, but Personal Worship becomes a *life-style*. Many would like to make Worship about *Positions* and *Postures* when it's really about *Relationship* and *Responsibility*.

*"It's my responsibility to Worship."*

As believers, it's our responsibility to Worship. Remember that the essential element in worship is that all who proclaim God as Lord must also be devoted to Him. Worship is the attitude of our hearts in fellowship with Him and is the result of our gratefulness for who our Lord Jesus Christ is, what He has done for you and me, and our commitment to express these essential qualities with an attitude of gratitude in both our daily lives and our church services.

The hub of Worship is Love. Love is defined as an intense feeling of deep affection.  The Bible has a great description of Love in ***Corinthians 13:4-7 New King James Version (NKJV), which states, Love suffers long and is kind; love does not envy; love does not parade itself, is not puffed up; does not behave rudely, does not seek its own, is not provoked, thinks no evil; does not rejoice in iniquity, but rejoices in the truth; bears all things, believes all things, hopes all things, endures all things.***

This is a very "self-less" description. This draws a line between *Religion & Relationship*.

In religion, you try to get right with God through your own human understanding. For example, you'll try to treat everyone right as you would desire to be treated, attend Worship services, and do special things to receive favorable consideration, etc. Reality states that building, having, and maintaining a relationship with God works much different. It's the difference between a guy that's in church thinking about fishing vs. a guy that's fishing thinking about God. That's *Relationship!*

Personally speaking, My Worship comes from the depths of my Deliverance. I will never forget the things that He's brought me out of and yet will continue to bring me out of. My *Deliverance* thus far by no means was pretty, so my *Delivery* ain't about being **cute**! I was headed down a road of ***Self-Destruction***. He cared enough about me to **change** the way I think, talk, and dress, the places I go to, etc. I can't name all the things that He's changed about me or else that would be this Devotional. His **LOVE** is Never Failing! He didn't walk away when He should have! He didn't stop loving me just because I didn't want Him, His work, nor to submit to His will. He had a Plan and a Purpose for me, and whatever He had to do to see that come to pass, He has done that and will continue to.

I often say that my heart breaks for so many because they act as if they have no clue of what love truly is and have never experienced it because of the way that they value love. Love becomes a chore when it's not valued.

I'm going to ask 2 questions as well as list an action item to provoke you to develop a closer relationship with the
Father:

> ➢ What's the hub of your Worship?
> ➢ Do you have enough attached to God to adequately *Worship* Him?

*(Sample Prayer)*
*Father, we thank you that you've graced us to facilitate worship in any facet. We thank you for choosing us to carry Your Glory. We repent for any time that we have misrepresented You.*

*Teach us how to properly love You and how to be devoted to You. Help us to see more and more of Your worth in our everyday lives. Open our eyes to see You more. Open our ears to hear Your still small voice and open our hearts to worship You more and more so that we may grow in grace and in the knowledge of our Lord Jesus Christ. Amen.*

# The Importance of Freshness
## *Chapter 2*

Have you ever found the worship services at your church to be dull or stale?  The songs seemed to have lost their effect and the congregants were either non-participatory or appeared to be unplugged?  Don't worry, it has happened to the best of us. In this chapter, we'll reveal the importance of obedience and relationship with our Heavenly Father to maintain Fresh Worship Encounters.

Leading Worship is one of the most frightening yet exciting and exchanging experiences. The responsibility of being led by the Holy Spirit, along with skillfully using your gift, and communicating biblically through song every week can be quite challenging, but certainly not impossible.

Worship Leading is bigger than us, our gifts and talents, and our appearances. The privilege to facilitate Worship shouldn't be taken lightly or for granted. It's imperative to remain close to God's Heart so that we can ensure freshness in our delivery of Worship. The core of Worship is "Surrender." The word "Surrender" is defined as one to stop fighting/resisting and to submit under the authority of another.

There is no way for us to know what each person needs from God in the congregation. You may think that the people are needing one thing just because that's what you rehearsed, but God may be speaking something totally different, but timely for that moment. God can speak one word and it'll be befitting to everyone in different areas of their lives.

Just imagine how you would feel if God spoke to you the day after you really needed to hear from Him. You'd most likely make the statement of, "If He had spoken this word to me the day before, it would've been far more effective." However, when we surrender to the leading of the Holy Spirit, we give space for God to Minister adequately to His People.

"How do you develop a sense of sensitivity to God's desires?"

This is a question that's asked by many worship facilitators.  One sure way to become sensitive to God's desires is through Prayer.  Communicating with the Father will strengthen your faith and trust to yield to His direction.
Proverbs 3:5-6 (KJV) states, Trust in the Lord with all thine heart, and lean not unto thine own understanding.  In all thy ways acknowledge him, and he shall direct thy paths.
Never should we ever become so comfortable in our gifts and talents to where we aren't depending on the leading of God's direction in Worship.  It's imperative that we seek God in every detail of Worship Planning so that we can be intentional about targeting exactly where God desires to exemplify His Presence.

*"Comfort breeds Complacency."*

You'll know that you've become comfortable with your Worship Presentation when you keep repeating the same set over and over again, when you're un-attentive to what God wants to do in an atmosphere, or you're constantly trying to recreate a past moment.  You may move the congregants, but you won't move God.  It's at this very moment where you've stifled the direction that God wanted to go in.  Being comfortable only affords you the opportunity to remain in circuits that ***applaud*** you and not ***challenge*** you.  Therefore, there will not be any ***change*** in you.

Obedience is the heartbeat of Worship Leading.  It's the vital component that produces the authenticity of the Presence of God.  Many like to make Worship Experiences about **Postures** and **Positions**, when it's really about **Relationship** and **Responsibility**.  Jesus was the Greatest example of obedience when He was here on earth; some of His greatest characteristics were servanthood, obedience, and humility. Jesus, in the Garden of Gethsemane, became quite weary, and in His flesh, He desired to reconsider fulfilling His assignment. Instead, He made a choice to be obedient, and said, "Not my will, but Thy will, be done."

We all are the better for His obedience in this moment, because of His steadfastness we've been Redeemed, and Salvation is available to all that believes. What if Jesus would've given up and chosen to be disobedient in the Garden? Your obedience can change someone's entire perspective about who God really is. Your submission to God in Worship could be the very Lifeline that someone needs, to live another day, to keep believing that God will answer their prayers, to believe that God will Heal and Restore them, etc.

*"You must stay FRESH."*

Let's kill the myth that people don't want God anymore. People will flock to the Authentic Presence of God. If people wanted a Corporate Experience, they have jobs for that. When the people of God gather, they want a God Experience. We must Prep for His Presence. Results ON stage Yield from being Responsible OFF Stage.

I'm going to list a question and an action item to provoke you to re-visit your relationship and obedience with our Father. To ensure that your delivery remains **fresh!**

*Are you wholeheartedly seeking God, or have you become comfortable operating in a "form" of Godliness?*

Evaluate your delivery to determine if it's stale or fresh. A recommended scripture to meditate on is, Proverbs 3:5-6 (KJV) states, Trust in the Lord with all thine heart, and lean not unto thine own understanding. In all thy ways acknowledge him, and he shall direct thy paths. This scripture will teach you how not to depend on your gift, but to depend on God.

(Sample Prayer)

Father, we thank You for gracing us to facilitate worship in any facet. We thank You for choosing us to carry Your Glory. We repent for any time that we have misrepresented You by not maintaining the freshness of our relationship with You. Draw us closer to You and grant us a mind to be obedient to Your will and to Your word. Fill us with Your Spirit and restore unto us the joy of Worship. We bless You for being The Almighty, All-Knowing, Amazingly Perfect Father that You are, and we thank You for the Victory in Worship. Help us to consider Your work as priority and let our Worship be a Lifestyle that glorifies You. In Your darling Son, Jesus' Name, Amen

# Having a Presence, Not Just Being Present

### *Chapter 3*

Your presence is your true identity. The word "presence" is defined as the state of being somewhere. It also reveals your demeanor and/or your bearing. In this chapter, we will unpack the importance of being present in the moment. Being fully present means having your focus, attention, thoughts, and feelings all fixed on the task at hand. Having a Presence and being Present is a simple thing to differentiate. After reading this chapter, you'll discover a more seamless way to journey through those moments in Ministry where your Presence is there, but you aren't Present.

*"Wherever you are, be all there"*

There are so many things in life that have the capability to shift our focus and throw us off our regular mental regimen. Reacting to our present feelings is so natural to do but isn't acceptable when we're a representation of someone else. It's incredibly disheartening when you have someone to represent you in any way and they embarrass you. My personal pet peeve is bad customer service. My motto is, "If you didn't feel like coming to work, you should've stayed at home." No one is going to say, "Customer service rep 83640, has a bad attitude," but they will say, "That COMPANY has bad customer service." It's the same way when we're representing Christ. When we're graced to Minister to God's People and we operate in our feelings, we misrepresent the love of Christ. If we were representing ourselves, that would be different. For example, you may be going through something in your home, on your job, in your body, etc. and you have to Minister; you're still expected to do that well.

"How is that Possible?"

This is only possible through our relationship with God. Experience and Maturity teaches us how to manage the placement of our feelings. This doesn't negate the fact that these are your true feelings; this just means that you choose to rise above your feelings and fulfill your duties in the right presence. I've ministered through sickness, depression, grief, etc. and didn't always understand the art of not being emotionally driven. I would just do what I knew to do just to get through that moment. I was there physically but wasn't there mentally. It wasn't until I began to yield myself and my emotions to God, and that's when I began to weigh my duty and calling over my present feelings. PSA! This was not a one-time lesson.

Prayer is essential in this matter because it disciplines you to proactively align your will with the will of our Father. If we don't control our emotions, they will lead us. The people of God will not be edified, and God will not be glorified. God has a standard of how He desires for His Presence to be represented. There are no 2 settings that are alike. Hence the reason why we must remain connected to His heart and mind to comprehend what He desires to deliver in each setting. We have different needs every day. One day, we need endurance to process through a challenging task. The next day, we may need a healing.

In the model prayer in *Matthew 6:11*, Jesus teaches us to pray and ask the Father to "give us this day our daily bread." This petition of the Lord's Prayer, then, teaches us to come to God in a spirit of humble dependence, asking Him to provide what we need and to sustain us from day to day.

*"Your plan without God's presence is a problem"*

Leading worship is not about our own agenda. God's plan must be the forefront of your Worship Planning and deliverance. Ministering out of self will cause you to stand alone.

Be watchful of the traps that are set by the enemy to shift your focus to a place where you can't Worship as God intends for you to.  Some of the most common ones are frustration, sound problems, people being out of place, etc.

These and other traps are planted to stiffen the move of God.  Your job is so important because people's lives are on the line!  Some come to hear a song and/or a word from God to leave better than they came.  If you're the chosen instrument that God wants to use and you're submitted to your emotions, how shall the people be edified? It does no one any good to come to a Worship Experience and the leader is physically there but is mentally and emotionally elsewhere. Being on stage is only a by-product of what's done off stage. If you have been in the Presence of God, you will bring that Presence with you and anything that you're facing in that moment, submission to God will discipline you to put "self" on the "shelf."

Steps to having a Present Presence:

Pray | Study the Word of God | Align your will with the Father | Grant Him permission to be the Lord over everything in your life.

I'm going to list a question and an action item to provoke you to re-visit your relationship and obedience with our Father to ensure that you're granting His desires.

"Are your emotions a Gauge or a Guide?"

Re-evaluate your everyday life so that what you are submitted to the most will be revealed: Your emotions or God?

(Sample Prayer)
Father, we thank You for gracing us to facilitate worship in any facet. We thank You for choosing us to carry Your Glory. We repent for any time that we have misrepresented You by being emotionally driven. Teach us how to properly handle Your Presence.

Help us to remain present through everything that we are facing. We give You full permission to be the Lord over our lives: We make You LORD of our spirit and hearts; we make You LORD over our mind, thoughts, and emotions; we make You LORD of our will and all our decisions; we make You LORD of our bodies, health, and the time and manner of our death; we make You LORD of our families, relationships, and friendships; we make You LORD of our businesses and work; we make You LORD of our finances, homes, and all our possessions; we make You LORD of our schedule and time; we submit to Your authority in every area of our lives and ask that You would come and fill us with Your Holy Spirit. Teach us who You are and how to walk in Your ways. We commit our lives into Your hands forever in Jesus' name. Amen.

# Serving Your Peers

## *Chapter 4*

Receiving help from someone is one of the most relieving feelings. The right kind of help makes the task tremendously successful. In this chapter, we will discuss what it means to serve. "Serving" is not a very popular word because it has a self-less meaning. It's defined as one who helps, assists, or aids others.

Jesus lived a life of humility. In *John 13:15*, Jesus sets an example for us to follow. After washing His disciples' feet, which was truly an act of love, humility, and service, Jesus says, "I have set you an example that you should do as I have done for you." He encourages us to follow His lead and serve one another.

Jesus, the Son of God, Lord of Lords, never placed Himself in a position above others. He led by serving, and He loved by serving. He washed feet. He fed thousands. He walked to visit and heal the sick and dead. He stopped to touch and heal a sick woman. He spent time with those no one else cared to spend time with, and the list goes on and on.

Jesus showed us that, being humble and serving others, partnered together, makes a great disciple, in which we all should be. Knowing how to serve generally, is a practice that is taught and learned over a course of time. Learning to serve your peers, puts an entirely different twist on serving, and is learned by intentional observation and submission. It's here where maturity rushes to the forefront of your character and displays servitude. Oftentimes, people miss the joy in serving their friends due to them not wanting to submit to their leadership, whether it's in one setting or continual. The definition of Friendship is simply an association between two people typically marked by similar things in common. Friendship was never meant to be a one-sided connection. It should always be about the exchange of serving one another.

Let's dig deeper into how to put this level of servitude into action. For example, if you're singing in the choir, praise team, on background vocals, or serving in any facet of Ministry and your friend is in a leading role, submit to their leadership in Humility and EXCELLENCE! I've seen so many scenarios of this matter being displayed. I've observed that some will exemplify a noticeable reservation of their gift until it's their time to lead. When it's in our serving, where we're creating a template of what we desire to receive. We don't have to always be in a leadership capacity. Matthew 23:11-12 teaches us that he who is really greatest will show his greatness, not in asserting it, but in a life of ministration.

### ******This is not about Friendship******

This is a time for you to, Pray for them! Pray for what they need in order to execute well. Pray that God will give them the strength, anointing, power, courage, confidence, and wisdom to know just what to sing and/or say. Pray for their minds that they will be able to focus on that, that God is trying to deliver through them. Pray that they will yield to the move of God and will be sensitive enough to shift, even if it's outside of their comfort zone. Pray that they'll be able to pour out beyond their pain or any life event that they may have going on. Pray that God would increase Himself within them so that He can be Glorified. Pray for them from a pure place, even if you disagree with some of their leadership choices. Respect the fact that they are in leadership and submit yourself to them as unto God. Not under any circumstance is this statement leading you to remain in a place that would be salvation crucial, but to be submissive to your leader, just as if you were doing it for God.

PUSH them! Don't allow them to remain comfortable, push them to be greater! Let them know and feel your support. Dress, accordingly, to what you've been asked to wear! STUDY & KNOW the material given!  If they ask you to sing or to serve in any way, that means they trust the GOD in your GIFT!  It's at this moment where you should BE the help that you'd want to receive! If the enemy uses anyone, don't let it be you!

Pray for the Atmosphere! This is where you'll have to be *pro*-active.  Please don't wait till it's time to serve before you pray for the atmosphere. Leading in any form of Ministry, singing on the Praise Team, the Choir, Background Vocals etc., it's your responsibility to pray for the atmosphere! Begin to invite God in.  Pray that the atmosphere is conducive for God to have His Way! Pray that all flesh be removed.  Pray against any level of confusion & strife. Pray against distractions and hinderances.  Pray against every plot and plan of the enemy that would come to deter the move of God.  Pray for all parties involved in the setting.  The singers, musicians, audio, video, media, ministers, etc. Pray for everyone who's destined to be in the audience. Pray that God will center their minds on Him. Pray that they receive everything that they need to continue their journey with Christ.

Serving is a huge responsibility. You must pray for yourself, that God will give you a mind to want to be submissive, first to Him, then leadership. There's no way that you're going to magically submit to leadership and don't submit to God. You'll learn more and more about how to submit to leadership as you allow God to capture and cultivate your character. Let's not make it *TOUGH* to serve each other in *Ministry*! *TREAT* and *SPEAK* to each other with respect, even in correction & frustration. It's a *Great Exchange.*

I'm going to list a question and an action item to provoke you to re-visit your relationship and obedience with our Father to ensure that you're serving your peers as unto God.

If you were in the place of leadership, and everyone else served as you did, what kind of support would you receive?

*Galatians 6:7*
*Be not deceived; God is not mocked: for whatsoever a man soweth, that shall he also reap.*

Many enjoy quoting this scripture typically when they're upset and is in a place of offense. However, the key word to this scripture is "that." It's the process of sowing and reaping. If you sow submission, "that" shall you also reap. If you sow contention and confusion, "that" shall you also reap. Sow what you desire to receive.

(Sample Prayer)
Father, we first thank You for the opportunity to serve in any capacity of ministry. We repent for any time that we've served incorrectly. Teach us how to submit ourselves to You. Give us a mind to allow You to capture and cultivate our characters. Help us to be self-less

and know when to give of ourselves and be what we desire to receive. We thank You Jesus for living a life of humility and being the example that we can follow to be great disciples. We love and thank You for being the so caring, loving, and gracious Savior that you are. It's in Jesus' powerful Name that we pray,

Amen.

# Choir Members

*Chapter 5*

Singing in the choir was indeed my greatest joy growing up.  I started singing in what we called the "Tiny Tot" Choir, then the "Sunshine Band," next, the "Big Choir."  At that time, once you finally made it to the "Big Choir," your life was just beginning.  You were able to wear those robes and march down the aisle every Sunday, go out and sing at the evening services, and the greatest of them all, you get to participate in Choir Anniversary.  This was a Show Stopping Service that you had to bring your A Game! I grew up in a Baptist church, and we had our choreographed march that we'd prepared just for that Special Day! For me, singing in the choir was all about us singing my favorite song, wearing a robe, hanging with my friends, etc. I never saw my position in the choir as a leadership position.

## "Choir Members are Worship Leaders"

As Choir Members, we must also see that we are in a position of leadership. As well as understand that, in order to lead effectively in worship, we must come prepared spiritually as well as musically. We are to come to our place of service having walked with and worshipped God throughout the week, that we might be ready to invite others to join in corporate expressions of adoration. In today's time, many ministries have strayed away from having a traditional choir with the intent of progressive growth. However, just because something is thought of as "traditional," doesn't mean it's not *relevant* for the body of Christ today. There are so many reasons why having a choir is important. Some of those reasons are: having a choir gives opportunities for many members to serve. Not everyone knows what facet of ministry they would like to serve in initially; however, the choir can be an entry-level place to join and display teamwork. The choir also provides a multi-generational fellowship. In some ministries, the choir is the only space provided for several generations to serve together. Lastly, the choir helps to produce good congregational singing. God intended for Worship to be for all His people.

"Choir Members Are Valuable"

You are so important and so valued as a Choir Member.  Do not hold back just because you may not be on a mic.  Begin to see the importance of your position.  Don't take it lightly. Someone is depending on you to Minister well. Each Ministry is different, and you are required to fulfill the duties as such. Here's a short list of expectations, but you're not limited to just the ones that I list.

- *Pray Daily*
- *Be Sincere*
- *Be Prompt*
- *Be Prepared*
- *Communicate*
- *Do Your Best*
- *Improve*

"A view from the pew"

The Bible says in **Psalm 33:1, "Rejoice in the Lord, O ye righteous: for praise is comely for the upright."**

Take note that this instructs us to rejoice! Not sing solemnly. This scripture simply means that praise looks good on you! How many times do you think someone has looked at the choir and saw someone not smiling or appearing to not want to be in attendance? Be mindful that people are watching you sing. Whether you're singing joyfully or tearfully, these are precious moments God uses to bring His people closer to Him.

I'm going to list a question and an action item to provoke you to re-visit your relationship and obedience with our Father to ensure that you're granting His desires.

If someone were watching, you in service will they be encouraged or discouraged by your body language?

Ask God to show you yourself and help you to Minister well at all times.

(Sample Prayer)

Father, we thank You for gracing us to facilitate worship in any facet. We thank You for choosing us to carry Your Glory. We repent for any time that we have misrepresented You. Teach us how to take the position of a Choir Member as a Worship Leader.  Grant us the wisdom on how to devote ourselves to the duties of being a Choir Member.  I pray over the director and/or the Worship Pastor that they are openly and regularly affirming the Music Ministry and are seeking to instill esteem for the Ministry on the part of the congregation.  Thank

you for the Victory in this change and growth,
In Jesus' Name, Amen.

# Reservoir of Songs
*Chapter 6*

The word "Reservoir" is defined as a stored supply. In this chapter, we will discover the importance of having a reservoir of songs for Worship. In today's time, Gospel music has become so vast and there are so many different styles in this one genre of music to select from. After reading this chapter, you will learn the art of building your own reservoir of music.

Music is essential in the life of the church. It's the common thread throughout your typical Worship Setting, which is why the placement of songs is so important. Music literally sets the tone for the atmosphere of the room. For some, music is their escape or their release. Some may never listen to any plain words, but they will hear them through music.

*"Music expresses that which cannot be put into words and that which cannot remain silent"*

Leading Worship, simply put, is expressing the hearts of the congregation to God. For some, it's the only language that they'll comprehend. This further proves that Worship is not just about singing your favorite song. Music is used to express the heart and soul.  As Worship Leaders, it's our job to facilitate the atmosphere in the way that God desires for it to flow. We must remain versatile in our library of songs for occasions such as: Devotion, Praise & Worship, Hymns, Sermonic Selections, Alter Call/Invitation, Funerals, Weddings, etc.

"How is this possible in weekly settings?"

Worship Planning! This can become a tedious task, but there's no way around it, it's truly a part of the job. Thinking through what songs to select for Worship depends on several things, such as: the entire flow of the event, the sermon topic/series, the theme, the rules and restrictions of that house, acceptable or unacceptable songs, etc. All of which, should be considered when you're planning worship.   You don't want to be guilty of seeming to be all out of sorts in your song selections,  i.e., you start the service out singing about *Peter walking on water*; then *Paul and Silas in jail*, for offering; *I know it was the blood*, for sermon; *it is well with my soul*, but the Message is about Revelations. This is what I call a "seesaw service"; up, down, and all around.  A steady progressing flow has to be taken into consideration when planning Worship so that the outcome for God's people can be them having an Encounter in His Presence.   Build your worship sessions from the "takeaway" point.

"I have a mixed age group of singers and congregants. How do I plan Worship to where it fits everyone?"

You select songs that can be weaved together that everyone can relate to and participate in.  It's called "Bridging the Gap" between the age differentials and the genres of music, i.e., *Lord, you are good* (Israel Houghton), *You are good Lord* (Raytina), *Great Is Thy Faithfulness* (Traditional Hymn).  This is an example of the familiar, the new, and the traditional. Everyone has to leave with an experience of Him.

"Songs are received through your delivery"

You can't sing a song that's saying one thing, and your body language is indicating something else. Presentation is everything. To just sing a song is not enough, but to Minister the song, makes a total difference.  This is what I call persuasive singing.  For example, if you're leading an alter call/invitation song, you can't just sing it as if Christ isn't being offered. There are souls on the line.  Minister the song as if it's your last time seeing them, and their last invitation to Christ. Study the word of God so that you can weave applicable scriptures into your songs.  Remember, it's not a sermon, but substance.  Plan your work and work your plan.

I'm going to list a question and an action item to provoke you to re-visit your relationship and obedience with our Father to ensure that you're granting His desires.

"Are you willing to expand your search for applicable music to be more effective?"

(Sample Prayer)
Father, we thank You for gracing us to facilitate worship in any facet. We thank You for choosing us to carry Your Glory. We repent for any time that we have misrepresented You in Worship with our delivery, with our choice of song, and with our own agendas. Help us to become sensitive to Your heart and learn how to communicate that to Your people. Give us a mind to consider Your work as priority. Don't allow us to be slack and slothful concerning our approach to Worship Planning. Show us how to glorify You in all that we do. In Jesus' Name, Amen!

# The Great Triangle

(The Communication Between the Pastor, Praise
Leader, and Musician)
*Chapter 7*

The Relationship between the Pastor, Worship Leader, and Musician is a unique blend that takes a Spiritual Connection to even comprehend.  I call it The Great Triangle because each point is to be connected.  It's imperative that all parties understand the vision, and work in that direction.  Knowing the Pastor's heart will help you channel through Worship. At any time that I've served in the capacity of a Worship Leader, I would make time to communicate with the Pastor to thoroughly understand what their vision is in this capacity.  After getting that understanding, I would go and prepare from that discussion and return with a plan indicating what I feel they're trying to communicate through Worship.

"Don't just Execute the Plan.
Read the Moment"

No two moments are the same.  Every moment is to be strategically read with the knowledge of the vision and the sensitivity of the Holy Spirit.  As a Worship Leader, I've learned to study body languages and to be attentive to the atmosphere, so that I won't be caught off-guard, in case anything swiftly shifts.  I've served with many Pastors and Musicians and there's an unspoken form of communication that is developed in the moment. Not everyone's temperament is the same.  You must thoroughly take your flesh completely out of the equation, to remain focused on the present moment. The synergy between the three reveals all. Synergy is defined as the interaction of two or more organizations' combined effect, which is greater than the sum of their separate effects.

This means that the main focal point of every-one has to be the same, which is Jesus. A church can sense the health of the relationship between the Pastor, Praise Leader, and Musician. When all leaders are unified, respecting what each other provides, there's no end to what God can do.

"Cease Worship Wars"

We've all experienced the underlined or out-landish Worship War between the Pastor, Worship Leader, and Musician. Mark teaches us that, "If a house is divided against itself, that house cannot stand" (Mark 3:25). Mutual respect and love will bring the understanding that's needed. Strive to work towards the will of the Father together in the Spirit of meekness. I would love to tell you that this is a simple fix, and everything will go smoothly forever, but that's hardly the case. Fact is, this can be a Triangle of war, but such misunderstandings have to be addressed. I've provided a Reference

Chart for a quick view so that you can see what this war looks like in plain view.

If the Pastor is Unappreciative - The Worship Leader feels Devalued.

Scripture Reference - I Thessalonians 5:15 - See that none render evil for evil unto any man; but ever follow that which is good, both among yourselves, and to all men.

If the Pastor is *Lording* instead of *Leading* – The Worship Leader feels *Denigrated.*

Scripture Reference – I Peter 5:2,3 - Feed the flock of God which is among you, taking the oversight thereof, not by constraint, but willingly; not for filthy lucre, but of a ready mind;

Neither as being lords over God's heritage but being examples to the flock.

If the Pastor is *Outlandishly Speaking-* The Worship Leader feels *Humiliated.*

Scripture Reference - Proverbs 15:1 - A soft answer turneth away wrath: but grievous words stir up anger.

If the Pastor *Gossips* about the Worship Leader – The Worship Leader feels Betrayed.

Scripture Reference - Proverbs 11:13 - *A talebearer revealeth secrets: but he that is of a faithful spirit concealeth the matter.*

If the Pastor has poor *Communication*- The Worship Leader feels *Uninformed.*

Scripture Reference - John 12:35 - Then Jesus said unto them, yet a little while is the light with you. Walk while ye have the light, lest darkness come upon you: for he that walketh in darkness knoweth not whither he goeth.

"Now let's see the OTHER side of it"

When the Worship Leader is *Lazy* - The Pastor feels Cheated.

Scripture Reference - Proverbs 18:9 - He also that is slothful in his work is brother to him that is a great waster.

When the Worship Leader is being a *Show-Off* – The Pastor feels Embarrassed.

Scripture Reference - Proverbs 11:2 - When pride cometh, then cometh shame: but with the lowly is wisdom.

When the Worship Leader is *Usurping Pastoral Authority* – The Pastor feels Undermined.

Scripture Reference - Hebrews 13:17- Obey them that have the rule over you and submit yourselves: for they watch for your souls, as they that must give account, that they may do it with joy, and not with grief: for that is unprofitable for you.

"Musicians introduce Music as Ministry to the Congregation"

Musicians are such an intricate part of Worship and are classified as Worship Leaders as well.  The Bible explains that every good gift comes from God (James 1:17). Music is one of God's good gifts. It shifts moods and atmospheres. Through music, we realize that we are to *Worship* with an awareness of what's happening in Heaven, so we are to *Lead* with an awareness of what's happening on earth.  For truly, if there's no *Ministry* in the music, then the music has no *Meaning*. Musicians, you are valued, needed, loved, and we *honor* you in this chapter.  Your contribution to Worship is remarkable.  Thanks for all that you do.

"Alone, we can affect a few. But together, we can change the world." - Jen Hatmaker

Musicians are expected to lead Worship, and by doing so, you must come on time, prepared, knowing your given material, dressed according to the attire that's assigned for that setting, with a great attitude, and have prayed and been before God.  For we all are Worship Leaders!

I'm going to list a question and an action item to provoke you to re-visit your relationship and obedience with our Father to ensure that you're granting His desires.

"Am I being a Partner or a Problem in the Great Triangle?"

Search your heart and your conduct and ask God to reveal yourself to you to see if you're contributing *Partnership* or you are the *Problem.*

(Sample Prayer)

Father, we thank You for gracing us to worship in any facet. We thank You for

choosing us to carry Your Glory. We repent for any time that we have misrepresented You.

Teach us how to intentionally build lasting relationships between The Pastor, Worship Leader, and Musician. Bind us together as one in the realm of the Spirit. Cause us to be sensitive to The Holy Spirit. Give us a plan for Worship that Glorifies You! Help us not to give into Worship Wars, for truly a house DIVIDED against itself, will NOT stand. We REPENT now, God. Please forgive us. Reveal ourselves to us and teach us how to grow forward in You. In Jesus' Mighty Name, Amen.

# Worshiping While Hurting

(Hurt in the church)
*Chapter 8*

Hurt of any kind doesn't feel good and it's accompanied by a pain that has no promised expiration date.  Some even say that emotional hurt can be so strong that it feels just as bad or worse than physical hurt. Hurt is seemed to be heightened when it occurs in the church. There are two reasons why I believe this statement is true. One reason is because the level of offense is magnified in church, and we can be guilty of being such a victimized people. The other reason is that the church is believed to be a safe haven, a place of refuge or security. This does not alleviate the church from having hurt people nor doing hurtful things.

"There is NO Perfect Church."

Oftentimes, many will jump from church to church striving to find a "perfect" church. There is no such place. The church is made up of all sorts of people from all walks of life. Offenses will come, but the method to handling them is through prayer, conversation, forgiveness, and healing. Too often, we hold each other to a "higher standard" of living, when everyone is held to the same standard. We're all expected to live according to the standards that God has set for us through His Word. We experience hurt on our jobs, but we're there every day. So why is there any difference when you're hurt in church? It's the same in your family, with a stranger, etc.

In Jeremiah 3:15, God is expressing His love towards the children of Israel by saying, *"And I will give you pastors according to mine heart, which shall feed you with knowledge and understanding."* This applies to us today. When searching for a Ministry to serve in, the first thing to do is to pray and seek God. Following the hype will not help you. God knows just where you need to be for your soul to be nurtured properly. Serve in your Ministry as unto God and not man. I believe that's one of our biggest hang-ups. Our aim should be to glorify God. Reality states that there will be hurt in church. Some really cruel things can happen in church. Your spirit can become quite wounded, and if you allow it, it will stiffen your desire to even attend and much less participate in anything concerning church. However, everyone must process through life and hurt is one of those processes. You will not live this life without being hurt. You just have to learn how to manage yourself when you are hurt. At times, being hurt is good for us.

"Some of my best growths came out of my worst hurts"

Oftentimes, some stuff must break up, for it to begin to grow. Whenever you're going to plant anything, you have to break up the ground so that the seed can be planted. This mirrors our heart. In (Hosea 10:12), the expression, "Break up your fallow ground" means, "Do not sow your seed among thorns," i.e., break off all your evil habits; clear your hearts of weeds, that they may be prepared for the seed of righteousness. Land was allowed to lie fallow that it might become more fruitful; but, when in this condition, it soon became overgrown with thorns and weeds. The cultivator of the soil was careful to "break up" his fallow ground.

Most people will acknowledge the hurt, allow it to stunt their growth, stop attending church, and never give the proper attention to their healing. I've learned that Hurt needs **Attention** and Healing needs **Help**. How will you know what type of care you need if you don't give your *hurt* any *attention*? If someone falls and scrapes their knee, you have to look at the wound to decipher what level of care that wound requires. Cleaning, Band-Aid, stitches, etc. But if you don't tend to that wound, it will become infected from the inside out and a greater consequence will then occur all because you didn't give your wound the proper attention.  Our hearts are the same. We'll harbor the hurt and pack around our unforgiveness like a newborn baby in a car seat.  God is committed to reconciliation.  He has given us instruction on how to handle offense in *Matthew 5:23&24 which states, Therefore if thou bring thy gift to the altar, and there rememberest that thy brother hath ought against thee; Leave there thy gift before the altar and go thy way;*

*first be reconciled to thy brother, and then come and offer thy gift.*

*"Getting it right is better than being right"*

God gets more Glory out of the situation when we strive to get it right with each other, as opposed to being at odds. Is it easy? NO! Will you have to swallow pride and ignore your ego? Yes! Will you have to repent? Yes! Will you have to forgive? Yes! This is how you rise above offense and allow God to mature you in this area. There's another twist to being hurt in the church. You are still required to worship, while you're hurting. Your hurt does not excuse you from your responsibility. Neither does it gives you a right to use your platform as an opportunity to lash out and respond directly or indirectly to your offense. When you're emotionally hurt in the church, you have to police your flesh. When you choose to give your offense to God and yet serve in a pure place, God honors that, and will remove the stench and residue of your hurt to where you don't even feel it anymore. #Witness.

"Give the Grace that you desire to receive"

One of my favorite confrontations in the Bible is the one between Nathan and David.  Nathan confronted David concerning his misuse of Bathsheba, "Uriah's wife," by using a parable of one

rich man and one poor man. The rich man had an exceeding amount of flocks and herds. But the poor man had nothing, except one little ewe lamb, which he had bought and nourished; and it grew up together with him and with his children. It ate of his own food and drank from his own cup and lay in his bosom; and it was like a daughter to him. And a traveler came to the rich man, who refused to take from his own flock and from his own herd to prepare one for the wayfaring man who had come to him; but he took the poor man lamb and prepared it for the man who had come to him.  When David learned of this, he became VERY upset and declared that, "As the Lord lives, the man who has done this shall surely die! He shall restore fourfold for the lamb, because he did this thing and because he had no pity." Then Nathan said to David, "You are the man! Thus says the LORD God of Israel: 'I anointed you King over Israel, and I delivered you from the hand of Saul. I gave you your master's house and your master's wives into your keeping and gave you the house of Israel and Judah. And if that had been too little, I also would have given you much more! Why have you despised the commandment of the LORD, to do evil in His sight? You have killed Uriah the Hittite with the sword; you have taken his wife to be your wife and have killed him with the sword of the people of Ammon." We all know what comes next, David becomes *REPENTANT* and *HUMBLE!* For he knew that he had sinned before The Lord! *He DID NOT GIVE GRACE* until the *"TABLES TURNED!!!"* In the end, his child did DIE, The Sword NEVER left his house, BUT God put away his sin, *Blessed* them, and showed them mercy! *Extend Grace* and *Mercy*! You Will Need It! Tables DO Turn! Make room for people to grow, even you!

I'm going to list a question and an action item to provoke you to re-visit your relationship and

obedience with our Father to ensure that you're granting His desires.

"Will you continue to Worship while Hurting?"

Search your heart and ask God to reveal the things that you may have suppressed or have been freshly wounded with and submit them to Him.  Expect a Healing through your Process.

(Sample Prayer)

Father, we thank You for gracing us to facilitate worship in any facet. We thank You for

choosing us to carry Your Glory. We repent for any time that we have disappointed You by worshiping with an incorrect attitude and spirit. Teach us how to continue to Worship through our Hurt.  Help us not to allow our hurt to stagnate our growth in You.  We repent for each time we have chosen not to offer self-less

Worship.  Keep Your grace ever before us in Jesus' Name, Amen.

# "Relationship with God"

## *Chapter 9*

What does it mean to have a relationship with God? This question has been asked by many. In this chapter, we'll define and discover the depths of having a relationship with God. The word "relationship" is defined as, the way in which two or more people regard and behave toward each other. In today's time, with the influx of selfishness, most relationships are one dimensional and are based on what one can receive from the other. Relationships were designed to be a partnership and cannot be developed overnight. Because the idea of having a relationship with God has been so OVERLY complicated by many, people think that it's not within reach. God's love is communicated by a numerous amount of people, all of which is from their experiences of Him, hence why having your own relationship with Him is imperative.

When I was a little girl, I used to watch my parents serve and love a God that I knew nothing about, until I had my own experience with Him. I basically went to church just to sing in the choir and fellowship with my friends. I didn't come to church to know God, nor have a relationship with Him. I honestly didn't know that I needed to have a relationship with Him, because all I had was religion.

*"How do I develop a Relationship with God?"*

A relationship with God is the most important relationship that you could ever have. With any two typical people, developing a relationship is a process, and it is weighed by worth. With God, it's just the same. God loves you and is already in to you. He loves us so that He gave His only begotten Son, to be the ransom for our sins. (John 3:16). We have to catch up to the idea of His love for us. Before we were even born, He already loved us. Conversations with God are a great entry level way to build consistency. Then create Relational habits. Not Eventful Habits, but Relational Habits! Anyone can enjoy a relationship that's filled with outside entertainment, but what happens when the entertainment is over?  What's the identity of the relationship, outside of where the attention has been placed?  Allow the Bible to be the place where God meets and speaks to you, then allow the Bible to be the place where you speak back to Him. The relationship builds in this form of conversing. Him to us, and us to Him.  Investing in a Relationship with God is the only way that you can truly comprehend what, how, when, or why He's so infallibly deserving of such Worship.

"Relational Worship"

True relational worship is allowing His Spirit to penetrate us, and we experience an exchange with Him, our hearts pouring out to Him. Religion alone doesn't have this level of reach, because it caps. **Religion** is just a **Role,** meanwhile **Relationship** is **Reality.** Whatever **Reality** you'll face in life, ***Relational Worship*** will carry you through it.

## "Your Relationship with God is Individualized"

No two relationships are alike. Never allow extremely religious, traditionally indoctrinated, legalistic church people, cause you to feel inferior about your love for God, nor turn you into someone God never intended for you to be! Allow God to reveal Himself to you how He desires to. God's word is enough, without the opinions of people. Love God with all of your might! Love Him with all of your heart, your soul, and your mind. Submit to Him! Read His Word.

I remember praying and vulnerably stating to God that I just didn't know how to adequately have a healthy, consistent, relationship with Him, because all of my relationships failed, and I viewed having a relationship with God, just as I did with man. I was so broken and watched everyone around me have a relationship with God that seemed to be going so well.  Because of what I was going through, I figured I wasn't ready enough, fixed-up enough, stable enough, to come before Him.  I told Him, "I just don't know what to say."  I'm supposed to be so strong and Minister to everyone, but I'm a MESS! How do I love You like this?

He said, "Say to Me what you would want to hear when you wake up in the morning."

Whew!  I woke up worshipping Him like it was my last chance.  From that, an even deeper relationship formed. Consistency is Key! Nothing has to happen tragically for you to begin a relationship with God.  Just start today! He's been ready to receive you. He's SO consistent. Sketch your own blueprint to your individualized relationship with God.

I'm going to list a question and an action item to provoke you to re-visit your relationship and obedience with our Father to ensure that you're granting His desires.

"Are you Personal or Impersonal with God?"

(Sample Prayer)

Father, we thank You for gracing us to facilitate worship in any facet. We thank You for choosing us to carry Your Glory, but we dare not be more interested in doing Your work than being interested in You.

We repent for all the times that we didn't give You the proper attention and obedience that you require. Raise an awareness deep down on the inside of us, that would cause us to desire more of You. Set a hunger and thirst within us that'll stabilize our focus on You.

We repent for every time that we have misrepresented You.  Have mercy on us, oh God, according to Thy loving kindness and according to the multitude of Thy tender mercies.  Blot out every transgression, in the Name of Jesus. Wash us and shape us into who You've called us to be.  Teach us how to love You, oh God. Teach us how to be disciplined disciples so that when men see our good works, you will get all the Glory.  Let our relationship with You compel someone to come to Christ, seeking what they might do to be saved, in Jesus' Name, Amen!

# A Call to Salvation

*Chapter 10*

I can't take for granted that everyone who reads this book is saved. In fact, I personally, asked God to allow this book to be attractive to the unsaved so that they can get a 2-for-1 deal. The door can be opened for someone to be healed as well as for them to be saved. Now before you get turned off, flip the page, or think that I'm getting too spiritual on you, just indulge me for a moment and I'll be sure to get straight to the point.

See, there's one thing that stands in the way of us having a relationship with God, which is SIN. You see, God had this idea of life in Paradise until Adam disobeyed Him and caused sin to enter the earth. SIN is something we all have in common because we were all born with it because of the disobedience of Adam, the first man. We were all born separated from God, which indicates a need for a Savior! You may ask, "Why do I need Salvation?" The answer is, because "Good Deeds" alone aren't enough to spend an eternity with God. Serving in Ministry alone isn't enough. Hence the reason why we need Salvation. Salvation is quite simple; it's just the deliverance from sin and its consequences. The benefit package of Salvation is second to none! The Health, Life, and Retirement Plan is unbelievable. You can refer to what I like to call "Life's Manual," The Bible.

(Simply put, Basic Instructions Before Leaving Earth) for the itemized listings of all the benefits that Salvation offers.

Just to name a few highlighted daily benefits:

> Day-to-Day Brand New Mercies Given – *Lamentations 3:22-23*
> 24-Hour "Eye Watched" Surveillance – *Psalm 121:4*
> 24-Hour "Body Guard" – *Isaiah 41:10*

Come on, who can beat that? Not to mention those are just "some" of the benefits.

By now, I'm sure you're wondering, "How is it possible for anyone to attain such Salvation, if Adam really messed things up for everyone?"

Great Question!

Gods' Love is so Massive for us, that He gave His only begotten Son, Jesus! Which means that you can still receive Salvation and God will receive you through His Son, Jesus! He was the only acceptable and ultimate sacrifice that God would accept for the Redemption of the world's sin. Therefore, Jesus came into this world not to condemn it, but so that the world, through him, might be saved. Long story short, Jesus had to come so that mankind would have a Mediator, to reconcile us to God, to become a ransom for many, to forgive us of our sins, etc. just to name a few.  Many may debate this fact and don't see a need for God, His Son, nor their Salvation.

When in fact none can argue that they're perfect always. If honesty prevails, the Bible is quite factual when it states, "For all have sinned and come short of the glory of God" Romans 3:23. We've all fallen short of God's standards that He designed for us to live by.

Obviously stating, everyone could use a little help with this thing called Life. Right where you are, you can be saved! It's just that simple. He's completely worth the try. Just invite Him in. Jesus wants to enter your heart today.

Yes! Today! Right now!

Better late than never! I know you may not understand everything as of now, but trust me, once you accept Him into your heart, this will be the greatest decision you'll make in your entire LIFE!

Hey, I'll even help you. Here's an example prayer that will assist you in knowing what to say when you talk to God, but feel free to pray your own sentiments from your heart. Once you take this step, the Spirit of God will come to live in your heart forever.

(Sample Prayer)

God, I confess that I have sinned, and I know that sin will keep me apart from You forever. I realize there is not one single thing I can do to earn my way into Your kingdom, not even all my good deeds. I'm believing in Jesus' death on the cross, His burial, and resurrection from the grave as payment for my sin. I receive Jesus as my personal Lord and Savior, and I devote my life to You. Thank You for forgiving me and giving me Your Holy Spirit, I'm forever grateful. I seal this prayer in Jesus' Name. Amen.

If you prayed this prayer or a similar prayer today –  HAPPY SALVATION BIRTHDAY!!

You can now relax in the assurance of having a never-ending relationship with God, and spending eternity with God! God created you, loves you, and desires to have an intimate relationship with you as your loving Father.

I'm rejoicing with you today because I know that is the most important decision that you'll ever make in your entire life! If you asked Jesus to come into your heart and save you today, please don't stop there. Pray and ask God to show you how to live for Him so that you can be a living example of His Love. Then, seek direction to find the best local ministry that you can serve in so that you can share your experience of God and introduce Him to others. *Remember, leave no **Soul** behind!*

## Lamentations 3:22-23

*22 It is of the Lord's mercies that we are not consumed, because his compassions fail not. 23 They are new every morning: great is thy faithfulness. –*

## Psalm 121:4

*4 Behold, he that keepeth Israel shall neither slumber nor sleep. –*

## Isaiah 41:10

*10 Fear thou not; for I am with thee: be not dismayed; for I am thy God: I will strengthen thee; yea, I*
*will help thee; yea, I will uphold thee with the right hand of my righteousness. –*

## Romans 3:23

*23 For all have sinned, and come short of the glory of God; -*

# <u>Notes</u>

# Notes

# <u>Notes</u>

# Notes